158.2 Ban

Banks, A.
Wrong feet first.

PRICE: $22.95 (3559/go)

wrong
feet
first

wrong feet first

A Gift of Stories for Your Inside-Out Kind of Day; by Artá D. Banks

© 2001 by Artá D. Banks. All rights reserved. Published in 2001 by Lovegifts Publishing

Lovegifts Publishing P.O. BOX 201388; Denver, Colorado 80220

www.lovegiftspublishing.com

Cover & interior design / production ©2000 Brian Taylor, Pneuma Books: Complete Publisher's Services For info, call: (410)287-1235. http://www.pneumadesign.com/books/info.htm Set in Adobe Bell MT 11½ | 14 pt. Titles set in Democratica with quotations in French Script.

Editor: Nina Taylor, Pneuma Books. Front bookjacket photograph ©2000 Brian Taylor, Pneuma Books. Photographs on pp. 6, 58, 66 and bookjacket back and sleeve ©Katy Tartakoff, The Children's Legacy.

Second Printing. Printed in the United States of America by Thomson-Shore, Dexter MI

08 07 06 05 04 03 02 01   9 8 7 6 5 4 3 2

Publisher's Cataloging-in-Publication
(*Provided by Quality Books, Inc.*)

Banks, Arta D.

    Wrong feet first : a gift of stories for your inside
out kind of day / by Arta D. Banks. — 1st ed.
    p.cm.
    LCCN: 00-191449
    ISBN: 0-9702601-1-3

    1. Interpersonal relations—Anecdotes.
2. Inspiration—Anecdotes. 3. Spiritual life—Anecdotes.
4. Family—Anecdotes. 5. Conduct of Life—Anecdotes.
I. Title.

HM1106.B36 2001   158.2
                    QBI00-789

wrong
feet
first

a Gift of Stories for Your
Inside-Out Kind of Day

Artá D. Banks

Lovegifts

This book is dedicated to
my wonderful children —
Nehemiah, Nicole, Kathryn, Kaleb, Karmen, and Nicholas
and to my grandparents
my mom and dad
and
to all the people who have experienced
inside-out, wrong-feet kind of days.

table of contents

Table of contents

Dreams & courage

Afterwords

Prosperity is a great teacher;
adversity is a greater one.
Possession pampers the mind;
privation trains and strengthens it.

—Hazlitt

foreword

$\mathcal{Y}$ou and I live in the same world as Arta Banks. But she sees it all differently than most of us do. Arta makes the extra-ordinary seem possible, and draws life-changing lessons from the mundane. As others have done, I have often read Arta's "lovegifts" and urged her to publish. At last she has.

Like her life, the stories that Arta writes touch my heart. They are to be savored and read aloud. It isn't just the integrity of the words, but her convincing hope that shines through to inspire and instruct.

Arta teaches her children and her friends to celebrate each moment of their lives. And through this book she opens a window to her secrets for thriving in a world that is often inside-out.

Dixie van de Flier Davis, Ed.D.
Executive Director
The Adoption Exchange

wrong feet first

introduction

When I was a teenager, I received many letters and cards from an adult friend. She would often write, "I'm sending this just because ..." or "I saw this and it reminded me of you." There was never any rhyme or reason to the wonderful lovegifts that arrived in the mail, but they always made a hard day easier and a good day brighter. Best of all, they always came just when I needed them.

About three years ago, I began receiving a lot of e-mail and the basic message was: "Tell me a story." I am not sure what was going on in people's lives that their hearts felt the need for a story, but I felt honored by their request and began sending stories every two or three months to the people on my mailing list. These stories became known as lovegifts because they were a gift from my heart to the people who

I care about. The people on my lovegifts mailing list began to share the stories with their families, friends, and co-workers. The stories had more of a positive impact than I could have imagined.

In sharing these stories with you, I hope that they will make a hard day easier and a good day brighter. I truly hope you will find a story that is just what your heart needed.

The stories in this book are true. Most come from my experiences of family life with my children, parents, siblings, and grandparents. Since these stories are not ordered chronologically, a bit of background is in order.

My adult life is perhaps not typical. Just a year after graduating with a nursing degree, I adopted my first child, Katie, at the age of nine months. I was, and still am, single. About two years after adopting Katie I added pediatric home care nursing to my work at a pediatric hospital. Then, a few months later in December 1991, I adopted a son, Kaleb, at the age of eight months. But that was only the beginning. Six months later I adopted siblings — Nehemiah, age seven, and Nicole, age five. In December 1993 I adopted another daughter, Karmen, at one week old. Then in December 1998 I gave birth to a son, Nicholas.

My experiences at home, as well as my professional experiences, have taught me two important lessons: life can be short and we all need love.

hope

*While there is life
there is hope.*
—cicero

Life's
Journey

I looked up to the sky and said, "God, I know you said you would never give me more than I could handle, but I think you have me mixed up with somebody else."

In 1993, I decided to adopt a fifth child — a newborn baby. Before this time, the youngest child I had ever adopted was eight months old, so I had missed the bonding time that came with nighttime feedings, the first tooth, and other milestones, like sitting up, crawling, and introducing solid food. The kids and I were so excited about the possibility of having a baby in our home and watching that child grow up.

Before I had completed my adoption paperwork, I found out about a little girl, not yet born but in need of a family. We were ecstatic. As we anxiously waited for her arrival, I had dreams about her. But nothing prepared me for the day I laid eyes on her. She was the most beautiful baby I had ever seen. Was she really going to be mine?!?

It did not take long for the kids and I to fall in love with the baby girl we named Karmen. She quickly became queen of our household, and it was not uncommon to find her siblings fighting over who would hold or feed her.

When Karmen was two-months old, our excitement turned to grief—she was diagnosed HIV-positive with a life expectancy of only two years. I went into a three-day depression. Everything was normal by day, but at night I cried myself to sleep—on the nights that I could sleep. I did not want my little girl to die. Parents aren't supposed to bury their children! I thought about all I would never see, including her high school graduation and her wedding day.

On the morning of the fourth day, I woke up and decided that I could spend her short life feeling sorry for myself or I could enjoy the time we had together. Scriptures I had memorized as a child began to flood my mind and provide strength and encouragement. I heard the voice of my father, who always told me that I am a Banks and that a Banks can do anything. I believed his words then, and I needed to believe them now. I thought of my mother and how strong and courageous she was, and that gave me hope.

I decided that anything we had to do for Karmen would be normal. If we had to go to the doctor five times a day, it would be "normal" and we would adjust. I decided that if I wanted to see her in a wedding gown, I would make her one. I realized although we may not see her graduate from high school, we could still celebrate every accomplishment in her young life.

With these thoughts in mind, we began our journey. The road has been rocky at times, but we continue to celebrate her life. We go tent camping with medical supplies in tow. We push her in her wheelchair as we hike along rocky paths. We cry at times, but often we laugh.

Sometimes, when Karmen is really sick, I get sad and feel lonely. One night when I was feeling this way, I began having a pity party —instead of my usual "can-do" attitude, I was thinking of how tough my life was. I looked up to the sky and said, "God, I know you said you would never give me more than I could handle, but I think you have me mixed up with somebody else." I instantly felt better. It was as if a huge load had been lifted from my shoulders. I had allowed myself to verbalize my humanness and it was a relief not to be supermom at that moment.

This journey we are on is not the one I chose when I decided that I wanted to adopt a baby, but it is the one I received when I fell in love with Karmen. I didn't have a choice about the fact that she is HIV-positive, but I am given a choice every moment to decide how I will respond to that fact.

Many times in life, we find ourselves in situations that are not what we wanted or anticipated. We must choose our response. We can sit around feeling sorry for ourselves, or we can face our challenges head on and make the best of them.

What will your choice be?

The photos on page 6 are of Karmen in the wedding gown made for her.

summertime
in my heart

What fire could ever equal
the sunshine of a winter's day?
—Henry David Thoreau

It was snowing outside when my children woke up and began dressing for the day. Kaleb, my four-year-old, came to the breakfast table wearing shorts and a T-shirt. I said to him, "Kaleb, have you looked outside? It's snowing. Winter is here!"

"But, Mommy," he said, "it's summertime in my heart!"

What situations in your life need to be looked at with a fresh perspective?

on becoming
a butterfly

*There are times in everyone's life when
something constructive is born out of adversity.*
—unknown

When I was in sixth grade, we studied butterflies. I was fascinated.
I believed the things I was learning in school, but I also needed to
observe them. I decided to do an experiment.

At home, I got out the *World Book Encyclopedia* and studied cater-
pillars. Once I had figured out what they liked to eat, I got an empty
shoebox, poked tiny holes in the top, and filled it with sticks, grass,
and leaves. I found a caterpillar, put it in the box, and hid it in the
backyard.

Each day I would come home from school and watch for any signs
of progress. I watched the process of the caterpillar forming a cocoon.
It was so amazing to actually see it happen. When the cocoon was
complete, it was hard, resembling the texture of a tree's bark. It hung

from one of the sticks I had placed in the box. I came home each day hoping to see the cocoon open.

I *really* wanted to see that butterfly.

It took several weeks for the much-awaited event to occur. I came home from school one day, and the butterfly had started to emerge. It looked like it was really struggling, but I did not try to help, because it would have ruined my experiment.

After the butterfly left its shell, it didn't fly immediately. "Perhaps it is resting," I thought. When the butterfly finally did take off, it was the most beautiful sight I had ever seen.

Years later I learned that the process of a butterfly struggling to come out of its cocoon is essential to developing wings strong enough for flight. The struggle works the extra moisture from their wings — the moisture needed to keep their wings supple inside the cocoon, so their wings can flex into shape when they are ready. After maturity, that same moisture makes their wings too heavy and limp to fly. If I had helped the butterfly come out of its cocoon, it would have never been able to take flight!

We sometimes have struggles in our lives that seem impossible to bear, but we must remember that we are preparing to fly like butterflies and our struggles are helping to build character. At times, we need to rid our lives of the things that weigh us down and prevent us from being all we can be.

The next time you find yourself in the midst of a struggle, remember the butterfly. It must struggle, too. But when the struggle is over, it takes full flight.

Spread your wings and prepare for an unbelievable journey!

What struggles, trials, or difficult times in your life have helped you become a better person?

celebrate your birth

Not flesh of my flesh
Nor bone of my bone,
But still miraculously my own.
Never forget for a single minute,
You didn't grow under my heart,
But in it.

—anonymous

ℳany people believe that Christmas is the day Jesus was born, so on that day, they celebrate. The Bible doesn't really tell us the exact day Jesus was born, but it does tell us about his birth and that because of His birth many lives have been touched. It is interesting to note that even the recording of time periods changed because of Jesus' birth. (B.C. means *Before Christ* and A.D., *anno Domini,* is Latin for *in the year of our Lord.*)

The greatest event for me this year was when I received phone calls from my parents (weeks apart and without collaboration) to tell me how proud they are of me and to tell me the story of my birth. I'm not talking about the "I pushed for a zillion hours story," but the story of what it felt like to become a mom and a dad (since I'm their firstborn).

This year, because of some sad events that happened in my life, I told my children the story of their adoptions. I shared what it felt like to be chosen to be their mom and how I felt the day I met each of them. It was by far the most powerful conversation we have ever had. Because of this conversation, Kaleb's favorite question, especially when he's in trouble, has become, "Mommy, are you still in love with my eyes?"

My children have always known they are adopted and the story surrounding their adoption, but they never really understood what all of that meant to me until this conversation. My parents made me feel like I could conquer the world, but I never understood how much I meant to them until our conversation this year.

I believe that each of us is born with a certain purpose in mind, and because of our birth the world is forever changed. Share the events of your children's births or adoptions with them — even your adult children. They probably need to hear it more than anyone else does. Share your thoughts and feelings about the news of their pending arrival and the first time you looked at them. I promise you that it will forever change the way they see you and the way they see themselves.

I was telling Nehemiah how he didn't even like me the first time he met me, and he said, "I didn't want you to know that, because I didn't want to hurt your feelings." He was amazed that I knew and that I still wanted to be his mom. He then told me I was his very first best friend.

When our children are young, we are their world. They want to please us, be like us, and be loved and accepted by us. I hear my children saying my words and using my gestures, and their love and admiration humble me. I pray that God will help us all to be good mothers and fathers, because the future of this nation depends on it.

This world would not be the same if you were not here. Remember that you are needed and you are valuable.

How is the world different because of you?

A boost back into the fig tree

A little help is better than a lot of pity.
—celtic proverb

When I was a little girl, my maternal grandparents had a huge fig tree in their backyard. My sister, brother, cousins, and I often climbed in this fig tree to play, laugh, and dream. We always had a wonderful time in that fig tree. The problem occurred when we had to come out. The sap from the fig tree made us itch, and we ended up feeling miserable afterwards.

Then my grandmother would draw our bath water and place us in the tub. After we finished bathing, she would rub our bodies with lotion and place us in front of a cool fan. We always felt much better after she cared for us.

The next day, forgetting our previous evening of misery, we would head back to the fig tree. When we came out of the tree, my grandmother would care for us again. The best part is that she never scolded us. She always provided the comfort we needed.

I think that life is much like the time I spent in the fig tree as a child. In life, we spend time playing, laughing, and dreaming with the people we love; but when life does not go as planned or when a tragic event occurs, it is like leaving the fig tree. We are miserable.

This is how it feels when Karmen, my youngest daughter, has to go to the hospital because of her chronic illness. A lost job, a diagnosis of terminal illness, death of a loved one, or a divorce may cause other people to feel this way, too.

I was lucky as a child to have my grandmother greet me and care for me as I exited the fig tree. But many people have no one to turn to as they face life's tragic events. People seem to disappear during these times — not because they don't care, but because they don't know what to do or say.

There are no magic words to make these situations go away, but friends who care can provide the comfort needed when a person exits the fig tree. Caring can be shown in many ways: hugs, phone calls, cards, letters, preparing a meal, e-mail, flowers, listening, holding hands, or sitting quietly together are just a few.

The important thing is not what you do or say, but that you do or say *something*. It can make all the difference in the world to someone you care about. They will feel as if their bath water has been drawn, lotion has been rubbed on their body, and they have been placed in front of a cool fan. It will give them hope that one day soon they'll be able to reenter the fig tree, and you will play and laugh and dream together again.

How can you comfort a friend when they come down from playing in their fig tree?

who you are matters

Children are likely to live up to what you believe of them.
—Lady Bird Johnson

This is a true story about a boy name Raymond. He was born on January 31, 1990, with full-blown AIDS and positive toxicology to several illegal drugs. Because his birth mother was unable to care for him, he was placed in foster care and everyone waited for him to die. He did not go to the zoo or the circus like other kids. He was going to die, after all.

When he was three years old, Raymond was unable to talk, or dress himself, or feed himself because he had had no stimulation. Everyone *was* waiting for him to die. But Raymond did not die, because he had a purpose on this earth. He was waiting for his angel.

She came to him in the form of an early childhood development specialist named Barb. Barb fell in love with Raymond on the day she

met him. Barb knew that the one thing Raymond needed most in his life — love — was missing, and she wanted to be his mommy.

Barb went to Raymond's social worker and said, "I want to be Raymond's foster mom. I want to take him home with me." The social worker said, "He's not worth the paperwork." The social worker was also waiting for Raymond to die.

Barb kept going to see Raymond, and each day it became harder and harder to leave him. Since his social worker refused to do the paperwork, Barb began banging on other doors. She got her house ready and, finally, she became Ray's foster mom. She taught him how to talk, feed himself, and dress himself. She showed him God's beautiful world. One day she took him to a pioneer museum, and they saw a pond. Raymond stood there in amazement and kept saying, "Wa, wa!" He was amazed because the largest body of water he had ever seen was in the bathtub. Barb also introduced him to the mountains and Raymond believed that God made them just for him. (I think he was right.)

One day, when Barb and Ray were enjoying the mountains together, Raymond said, "Mommy, you need to bring the kids here."

Barb asked, "What kids?" and Ray replied, "The kids with AIDS."

Barb looked puzzled and said, "But I don't know any kids with AIDS."

Raymond replied, "You will, Mommy, you will."

They had many weeks together after that conversation, and Ray had a positive impact on everyone who knew him. He loved cowboys, horses, Garth Brooks, the mountains, and his mommy. He was full of life, because his life had been filled with love.

On April 16, 1994, Raymond's hospital room was full of people who were there to say good-bye. Ray was four years old. Raymond's social worker came to say good-bye, and Barb told him, "Look at all the lives he has touched. Do you still believe he's not worth the paperwork?"

I never met Raymond, but he has touched my life and the lives of many others. His mother shared his dream of wanting kids with AIDS to enjoy life in the mountains. The people who knew and loved Raymond volunteered to make his dream become a reality. They work all year to raise money to fund Camp Ray-Ray, held one weekend each year for families infected or affected by HIV and/or AIDS. Because people living with a chronic illness often face devastating financial situations, this camp is free.

The first camp was held in 1995 on Memorial Day weekend, and our family was one of fifteen that attended. Karmen was so sick that medical personnel were questioning why I was taking her. However, none of the families at Camp Ray-Ray ever questioned why I brought this sick child to camp. They knew that I was trying to fit all the wonders of life into a few days. They understood my need to live every day to its fullest, because tomorrow is not guaranteed.

That weekend at Camp Ray-Ray was the first time since Karmen's diagnosis that I didn't have to worry about how to tell, who to tell, and how people would react. We were all able to just be, live, laugh, and love. We spent the weekend horseback riding, fishing, hiking, doing crafts, laughing, hugging, and relaxing. We all cried when it was time to say good-bye. The fifteen families had come to Camp Ray-Ray as strangers, but we left feeling like an extended family.

We are all worth the paperwork. When you get discouraged and wonder if you are making a difference in this world, please remember Raymond and know that what you do and who you are does matter.

Who have you written off?

I BELIEVE IN YOU

I want to tell you that I believe in you;

I believe in your mind and all the dreams, intelligence,

and determination within you.

You can accomplish anything.

You have so much open to you,

so please don't give up on what you want

from life and from yourself.

Please don't put away the dreams inside of you.

You have the power to make them real.

You have the power to make yourself exactly what you want to be.

Believe in yourself the way I do,

and nothing will be beyond your reach.

—Author unkown

For more information on Camp Ray-Ray, see the appendix.

community

When spider webs unite,
they can tie up a lion.
—Ethiopian proverb

making
ice cream

Life is much like making ice cream. There are times when we need to do the easy turning, and there are times when we are able to do the hard turning.

When I was a child, the fourth of July was my favorite holiday. On this day, our family gathered for good eating and homemade ice cream. We only made ice cream once a year, so it made the day even more memorable. The women brought the ingredients for the ice cream and gathered in the kitchen to mix them together. The children took turns turning the ice cream maker, and although the men took care of the barbecue, they also took over turning the ice cream maker when it became too difficult for the children. With the effort of the entire family, we had ice cream at the end of the day. It did not matter who had turned the most, who had bought ice cream mix instead of making it from scratch, or who had cut the most fruit for the ice cream. We had all done what we were capable of doing, and because of this we were able to enjoy the harvest.

I think that life is much like making ice cream. There are times when we need to do the easy turning, and there are times when we are able to do the hard turning.

On my way home from work one night, I stopped by the grocery store for milk and found myself making ice cream with strangers. The store was in an unfamiliar area of town, and I was a bit nervous because it was dark outside and the surrounding stores had burglar bars on their windows. I was concerned about my safety, but decided to venture in because I was too tired to find another grocery store. With my keys between my fingers, I walked from the parking lot to the grocery store.

I got my milk and proceeded to the checkout line. As I stood in line, I noticed a young mother with her baby. The child was small, but I could tell that he was older than his size indicated because of the way he was purposefully playing with and manipulating his toys. The young mother kissed, talked to, and held the little one with much tenderness and love. It was obvious that he was her life.

When it was the young mother's turn to check out, the cashier rang up her items. She was buying formula and diapers for her baby. When the total amount was presented, the mother realized she did not have enough money to buy what her child needed. She quietly began to put back the diapers and several cans of formula. As I watched her do this, my heart cried for her. I had never been in her situation before, but I could only imagine how awful it must have felt. I tried to figure out how I could discreetly help her. I did not have much cash on hand, and I didn't know how to use a debit card with discretion. I felt sad for her.

Apparently, others in the store noticed this young mother's plight because they began opening their purses and wallets and digging in their pockets. People began placing money on the counter. I followed suit. When all the money was counted, the mother had enough to buy two cases of formula and a pack of diapers!

People gave what they were able and willing to give, and a little boy went home with the items he needed to survive. It did not matter who had put in the twenty dollars or who had put in twenty cents. We all worked together, and when it was over there was not a dry eye in sight. We enjoyed the harvest of making ice cream together.

When have you made ice cream with others?

you're
a color too

*If you judge people,
you have no time to love them.*

—Mother Theresa

The summer before my fourth-grade year, my family and I moved into a new neighborhood. I was so excited. The backyard was paradise: abundant trees, manicured flowerbeds, and squirrels to watch from the patio window. It did not take long for my excitement to subside. You see, we were the first black family in the neighborhood, and we had planted ourselves in the middle of Ku Klux Klan territory.

"For-Sale" signs began to spring up. People egged our house and wrote obscenities. Some mornings we woke up to a yard full of garbage. I was nine years old, and I was scared. My dad would stay up at night, gun in hand, because he didn't know what people would do. I only felt safe when my dad was home.

When we began school, there were five black kids (and three of them were my siblings and I). We settled in and made friends. My sister's best friend was white. They sat together in class, ate together, and played together at recess. One day at recess, I found my sister Toni sitting on the playground and crying. Her best friend was not with her. I asked Toni what was wrong. She said that she was the only one who had not been invited to her best friend's birthday party. I asked her why, and she told me her friend's mom had said that Toni could not come to the party because she was colored. I put my arms around my sister and cried with her. We were sad the rest of the day.

When we got home from school, we tried to hide our sadness. We did not want our parents to know what had happened, but my mother knew something was wrong. When we finally told her, she said, "When you go back to school, tell your friend that she is a color, too."

Those were magic words that empowered us. My sister and I smiled. We went to school the next day smiling.

In the midst of all the prejudice we were facing in our neighborhood and at school, I never heard my parents say one bad thing about the people who were causing us so much grief. I'm not sure what kind of conversations they may have had in their bedroom, but I know that they never uttered one derogatory word in front of us. They understood that the acts of one group of people did not speak for the whole.

I learned an important lesson that day that has stayed with me all of my life. The lesson was that we are *all* people. Race, socioeconomic status, IQ, and the rest are part of who we are, but not *who* we are. Whether you are rich or poor, gay or straight, black or white, smart or not so smart, HIV positive or negative, male or female, stay-

at-home mom or working mom, all are valuable. When I look at someone, I do see their race, and perhaps discern their economic status,
but I am prepared to like them based on who they are and not those
other things.

Sometimes, we find ourselves judging people because they are different from us or we perceive them to be different from us. Today I
would like to challenge you to look at those who are different than
you — perhaps a kid in baggy clothes, someone with a tongue ring or
other unusual piercing, someone who is homeless, or a person you
may not ordinarily associate yourself with — and accept them just
as they are. Take the time to get to know them, and you will find that
they need love and acceptance just like you do.

When my kids and I discussed differences and our reactions
to people who are different, my daughter Katie, age eleven, wrote
this poem:

THE KIDS OF COLOR
Two little black girls walking by
Spotted two little white girls and tried to say "Hi."
They did not even budge, did not even smile.
One little black girl said, "It will take a while.
It will take a while for them to wake up and see
We are no different on the inside. They are just like
You and me."

Two weeks later, they try it again.
Two little black girls walking by

Spotted two little white girls and tried to say "Hi."

The little white girls said, "Why?

Why are you saying 'hi' to us?"

"Because we want to be friends. Let's not make a fuss.

We want to walk, read, and sit together on the bus."

Two little black girls walking by

Spotted two little white girls and tried to say "Hi."

They were greeted with a smile.

See I told you, it would only take a while.

The four became friends

And were happy to the end.

We hope you'll join our family in this challenge, because together we can eliminate the prejudices that separate us and embrace the fact that we are all valuable.

Who will you befriend?

the echo

*Kind words can be short and easy to speak,
but their echos are truly endless.*

—Mother Theresa

I have been a nurse for twelve years. This reality is astonishing to me because my first year out of nursing school was the most stressful year of my life. Many times I wanted to say and *did* say, "Forget it. This is for the birds." I investigated the possibility of becoming a doctor or lawyer instead. I knew I had options. Armed with this knowledge, I decided to give nursing one year, and if it didn't work out, I would return to school. There are a host of stories and lessons learned during that first year. I have carried them in my heart and tried to live them every day of my life. Here is one I wish to share.

I was twenty-three when I graduated from nursing school, an eager young woman full of hopes and dreams and ready to make a difference. I had been working for less than two months when a doctor came to the nurses' station and said, "Who's taking care of so and so?"

I noticed that every nurse at the desk froze as I walked up to him and said, "I am."

He began yelling at me, and I had no idea what he was saying or why he was so angry. I looked him in the eye and spoke in a voice barely above a whisper. He stopped yelling so that he could hear me and these were my words: "My parents don't even speak to me that way. When you are ready to talk to me like a decent human being, I will be in the nurses' lounge." I turned and walked away.

Within five minutes, that doctor was in the nurses' lounge apologizing. I told him that he was forgiven and asked him to sit down so that we could figure out what the problem was and fix it. It turned out that he had gotten himself worked up about something that did not even happen!

When I came out of the nurses' lounge, his colleagues (the ones who shared an office with him) were thanking me, and the nurses were smiling and happy. People were happy that this doctor had been put in his place, but that was not my intention. I had not been angry. I was merely in shock because no one had ever spoken to me that way. I never imagined that people spoke to each other like that!

I later learned that people were happy because this doctor yelled at everyone and they were glad someone had finally said something to make him stop and think. Since he had joined this medical office, it had gone from a pleasant, happy work environment to an office full of misery. When he came to the hospital to see his patients, the nurses would scatter (they froze on this day because they wanted to protect me). Everyone was miserable because of one person's behavior. It reminded me of a story I once heard and shared with every child I met one magical summer.

There once was a little boy who loved visiting his grandfather every summer in the Swiss Alps. Each day after doing his chores, the little boy would go exploring. One day he found a beautiful spot. It was high on the mountains, and there was a valley below. He thought it was God's most beautiful creation! As he looked down, he wondered if there were people below. He decided that if he shouted hello, someone would hear him and shout hello back and he would have a new friend. The boy shouted, "Hello" and the mountain said, "Hello, hello, hello." The boy realized that the mountain was echoing back to him, and it made his heart happy. He then shouted, "I love you" and the mountain echoed, "I love you, I love you, I love you," and the little boy's heart was really happy. The little boy continued to explore different places everyday, but this spot became his favorite. He would visit it everyday and shout "hello" and "I love you" and listen to the mountain speak to his heart. One day, the little boy got into a fight with his grandfather and ran off. He found himself in his favorite spot and he shouted "I hate you" and the mountain echoed, "I hate you, I hate you, I hate you." The little boy fell to his knees and began to cry, because this echo did not make his heart happy.

Have you ever considered that what you put out will come back to you? It is not always as immediate as an echo, but it will be returned to you. Today think about the things that make your heart happy and make an effort to give those things to others. I promise you that in time it will be returned to you tenfold.

What happy things echo deep within your heart?

Touching Lives
with Your Talent

If you think you're too small to make a difference, you've obviously never been in bed with a mosquito.
—Michelle Walker

Although it sounds odd, I spent most of my college life in the freshman dorm: first as a resident and then as a resident assistant. I had a new group of freshmen each year, and I never grew tired of watching them grow up and learn to live on their own. It was a refreshing time for me.

One of the perks of being a resident assistant is that I had one of the easiest jobs on campus — working at the front desk. My responsibilities included answering the phone, paging residents when they had a male guest, giving out the residents' phone numbers, and clearing the lobby at curfew.

I enjoyed this job. Many of the dorm residents would stop by to tell me about their day. I would be there when the guys came to pick up their dates, and I would help them with their ties or calm them down when they were nervous. It was a job that made me smile.

One night after working at the desk, one of the freshman girls came to my room and said, "Arta, have you ever noticed that when you are working the lobby is usually full, and that when you are not working the lobby is empty?" I shook my head no. She continued, "Well, it's because the guys like for you to touch them on the shoulder. If you are working, they'll stay in the lobby until curfew."

The usual practice was that about ten minutes before curfew, most of the girls who worked at the front desk would yell a warning to those still in the lobby that it was time to retire. But when I worked I would go to each of the boys in the lobby, gently place my hand on their shoulder, and tell them that it was ten minutes until curfew.

Wow! A tradition that I started because I didn't like yelling had made a difference in others' lives. I was just being myself—doing something that made me smile, and it was meaningful to others. We can each make a difference in someone's life simply by being who we are and using our natural talents.

Here is a good example. Katy Tartakoff enjoyed photography for many years. One day she decided that she wanted to use something she loved doing to help children diagnosed with cancer. She decided to help them create a legacy of pictures. Katy raised some financial support from family and friends and began what is now known as The Children's Legacy (TCL). TCL has helped numerous children tell their stories through the use of words, photographs, and drawings.

Some of my nursing patients have used her services, and I have seen the difference in their attitude toward themselves and their diagnosis. TCL touched their lives in a positive way.

When I saw these children and their families, I had no idea that any were using the services at TCL, but I noticed that some families were coping better than others. In the families that were coping well, the cancer patient's siblings were able to talk about the diagnosis. They also played with and interacted with the sick child as normal children interact with each other — arguing, teasing, wrestling, etc. The ill child was more interactive and willing to joke with and tease the nurses. They spoke openly about their diagnosis, but were also able to share their hopes and dreams for the future.

It was a few years later, when TCL expanded its services to include all children with terminal or life-threatening illness, that I realized why some children were coping better than others. My family became involved with TCL at that time and when we walked into the studio for a family picture, I noticed photographs of my former patients. I remembered the times I had shared with these children and their families and how I usually left their homes with a positive feeling. I knew then that TCL's involvement in their lives was the reason they coped better than some of the other families.

My children are coping better than many children in similar situations and I believe TCL deserves some credit for that. My son wrote the following words when he was twelve to express his feelings for TCL:

There are some days that you remember like no other:

The day I said, "Good-bye" to my birth mom and "Hello" to my forever mom.

I remember the day Mom brought Karmen home. I remember asking her if she brought home the right baby. She said, "Yes, and she's perfect!"

I remember the day Mom told us that Karmen had HIV. I was so sad. I would have jumped off a bridge, if it would have taken the disease away. I felt like I was in the dark and couldn't find the light.

I remember the day I found the light; it was the day I met TCL. We were at a family workshop, and we traced Karmen's body on a poster and cut out words and pictures to express our feelings. It was the first time we talked about HIV with laughter instead of tears.

I can now look at Karmen and see love instead of this horrible disease. I can now look at Karmen and say, "She's so beautiful. I'm glad she's my sister."

I would like to share a poem that I wrote for my sister last year:

> Karmen's sweet. She's full of love.
> She is so beautiful. She's like a dove.
> Our house is full of lots of love.
> When Karmen dies, we'll know she's above.

I want to thank The Children's Legacy for helping me find
the light!

—by Nehemiah Banks

A woman, simply by doing something she enjoyed doing, founded
TCL and touched people's lives.

We can all touch lives by using who we are and what we love to
make a difference.

What talents can you use to touch others?
Whose life will you touch with your talent?

For more information on The Children's Legacy, see the appendix.

A Cure for Loneliness

If I can stop one heart from breaking,
   I shall not live in vain.
If I can ease one life from aching,
Or cool one pain,
Or help one fainting Robin
Unto his nest again,
   I shall not live in vain.

—Emily Dickinson

A few years ago, several nurses and I were assigned to teach the family of a newly diagnosed cancer patient how to give their child intravenous nutrition and to help them understand her medication regimen. The home care team had visited this family several times already and were not making any headway. We had an informal case conference and decided that what this family needed was consistency.

Since Karmen was doing well, and I was a PRN (as-needed employee) with a more flexible schedule, I volunteered to do both the early morning and late evening visits for as long as it took to get this family educated. I decided to wipe the slate clean and begin teaching the family as if I had never been there before. We started at the very beginning.

After the third visit, the father was still resistant to learning or doing anything. I finally confronted him and said, " I know you love your daughter very much, because I can see it in your eyes. I also know that you are a very intelligent man. I am confused, because I don't understand why you are pretending not to understand what I am teaching you. Will you tell me what the problem is?"

The father looked at me and said, "I am afraid that if I tell you what I know, you will leave, and then I will be all alone."

Those words touched my heart, because I knew how he felt. Since my journey with Karmen began, I have felt alone more times than I care to count.

I wanted this father to know he was not alone, so I opened my nursing bag, took out a piece of paper and a roll of tape, and wrote the number for Children's Hospital Home Care Agency (my employer) three times. I tore off the first phone number, taped it to his shirt, and said, "This is the number for Children's Home Care. You are never alone."

I tore off the second number, taped it to his phone, and said, "If you ever have a question or a problem, all you have to do is call this number and someone will help you. They will even come to you, if you need it. It may not be me, but someone will help you."

I tore off the third number, placed it under his pillow, and said, "It's okay if you call this number in the middle of the night or the wee hours of the morning. Someone will answer the phone."

After this conversation, the father did all of his daughter's intravenous and oral medications and did them perfectly. I asked if he needed me to come and help him in the morning, and he said, "No."

I asked him if I could call him in the morning to check on them, and he smiled and said, "Yes."

I called the next morning, about one minute after her intravenous nutrition was due to be finished, and he had disconnected her from the intravenous machine without any problem. I went to visit one more time to make sure he had no questions, and that was the very last time I had to see them.

Many people have moments of fear and loneliness. We can change this by offering our ears and our phone numbers to those around us. Find at least one person to give your phone number to. It can be a child, a teenager, a co-worker who's going through a divorce, a friend who's had to put a parent in a nursing home, or a person you know who's going through a hard time but you've been avoiding because you don't know what to say. It can be anyone you choose. Write your number down three times and explain what you are doing. You can suggest they pin one to their shirt, tape one on their phone, and place one under their pillow.

If we all chose someone, no one would ever have to feel like this father did. Wouldn't that be wonderful?

Who will you choose?

Thank You, Mr. Bob

The bitterest tears shed over graves
are for words left unsaid and deeds left undone.
—Harriet Beecher Stowe

There are some people we meet who change our lives just by being who they are. I met such a person when I was twelve years old. His name was Bob Carpenter, but to the youth group at church he was known as Mr. Bob.

Mr. Bob was one of two men who oversaw the youth group activities at church. He was the bus driver for all the activities, and he also served as assistant director and handyman during the teenage session of summer camp. He was always open and willing to serve the teenagers in any way that was needed.

During my teen years, Mr. Bob's name became a household word. I liked him because he always made me feel special. Whenever there was a scheduled church event or youth group activity, he would always seek me out to give me a hug. He made me feel like a princess.

I've never understood why Mr. Bob chose me — I had a father, did well in school, and got along with my peers — but his kindness toward me made an enormous impact on who I am. When I chose to adopt children, I had planned to only adopt girls because I am single and there would be no male role model in the home. When a baby boy was presented to me, I thought of Mr. Bob and the wonderful things that he had done for me. I believed that there were other Mr. Bobs in the world and I knew that if this boy could have a Mr. Bob in his life, he would be okay! He would have the male role model that he needed. With this in mind, I brought my little boy Kaleb home.

Mr. Bob never knew that he was the reason why Kaleb had a place to call home or that he made me feel so special. He died before I had a chance to say thank you. When my mom called to tell me that Mr. Bob had died, I was heartbroken. The news came at the same time my youngest daughter was sick and in the hospital. I knew that I would not be able to attend his funeral to say good-bye. My heart was heavy with grief. This wonderful man would no longer grace the earth with his kindness.

My biggest regret was that I had never said, "Thank you." In honor of Mr. Bob, I decided then that I would always say "thank you" and let people know how much I appreciated them within twenty-four hours of the kind act. This simple act has been life changing, not just for me but for some of the people I have thanked.

When Karmen is sick and has to go to the emergency room or urgent care center, it is always stressful for us. There was a nurse at the urgent care center who seemed to understand this fact and made our visits as pleasant as she possibly could. She always made sure our visits were as short as possible; she explained what she was doing before she did it; she served as a liaison between us and the medical team; and she always made Karmen feel special by providing her with stickers, telling her how pretty she is, and taking extra time to talk to her. Whenever Karmen became ill and needed to go to the urgent care center, I found myself wishing that this nurse was working, because I knew that the visit would be less stressful — possibly even pleasant. I decided to write this nurse a note to let her know how much we appreciated her and how much Karmen liked her.

The next time we went to the clinic, the nurse said, "Thank you for your note. I was thinking about leaving nursing. I didn't think that I was making a difference anymore. Thank you for letting me know that I am."

An excellent nurse was thinking of leaving the profession because no one had ever taken the time to say, "Thank you. You're doing a good job."

We all have people in our lives who have had a positive influence on who we are. Taking the time to say "thank you" is a beautiful way to honor who they are and who you've become because of their presence in your life.

Thank you, Mr. Bob.

Is there someone in your life who you need to thank?

circle of kindness

Some words are like rays of sunshine, others are like barbed arrows or the bite of a serpent. And if hard words cut so deep, how much pleasure can kind ones give?
—John Lubbock

Each summer from ninth grade until my freshman year of college, I went to a summer camp, Camp Smiling Acres. We played volleyball, softball, ping pong, and badminton. We had shaving cream and balloon fights, played jokes on each other, and had cabin raids. We studied the Bible every day, sang a lot, and grew closer to each other. I always looked forward to this week of camp.

There was one event in particular that I liked. It was a tradition for the teenage session, and we did it on the last night of camp.

We waited until it was completely dark out and then the campers were divided into two groups: girls and boys. The two groups went to different areas of the camp. Everyone received an unlit candle and joined hands to form a circle. An adult counselor usually started the event by lighting her candle and choosing someone in the circle that had touched her life in some way that week. She would tell that person what she appreciated about them or what they had done that was meaningful, and then she would light their candle. The adult counselor would rejoin the circle, and the person she had selected would choose someone else. When the event was complete, everyone was shedding tears of joy. In just a few short hours, the night had gone from darkness to light.

There were always several people in that circle that I could have spoken kind words to, and I know that most of the teenagers felt the same way. Yet it took an event for us to express our positive feelings toward each other. We felt loved and encouraged after all the candles were lit, and we were all connected by the power of kind words.

Kind words do have the power to change people. An example of this occurred when I was in eighth grade. My sister Toni and I went to the same school. Each morning, we waited at the bus stop with our friends.

One girl at the bus stop was different. I'll call her "Michelle". She was rude, conceited, and talked to herself. Michelle had an attitude bigger than the state of Texas. She was not well liked and no one ever sat with her on the bus. People talked about her and told jokes at her expense. My sister and I had a hard time being around her, but we often discussed how to be friends with Michelle.

One day, Toni and I were sitting in Bible class and the teacher read a verse in the Bible that talked about being kind to your enemies and how that could bring about change. Toni and I looked at each other and said, "That's it!" The next day we began to show kindness to Michelle. We smiled when we spoke to her and we sat with her on the bus. We did these things regardless of her response.

Within two weeks, we were riding on the bus with a nicer Michelle. She smiled when she saw us. I no longer felt as if she thought she was better than I was. Through kindness, we had brought light to a lonely person. We were connected.

Later that year, I witnessed Michelle becoming friends with another lonely girl. She continued the circle of kindness.

Whose candle will you light with kindness today?

The Gift of
Mentoring

We all have something to give.
We all have something to teach.

$\mathcal{T}$he church I attended as a teenager had a tradition of taking a trip to Pensacola, Florida, each summer for vacation. The families stayed together in condominiums or hotels on the beach, and no family or individual was denied access to this trip due to a lack of money. Those who had much shared with those who had little. We cooked, ate, sang, and played together. It was a time that I looked forward to each year.

Each morning, a group of people, usually teenagers, gathered together to go water skiing. Two men from church drove the boat and supervised the activity. I had never tried to ski, but one morning I decided that I wanted to learn. After getting some instructions from my peers, I got my life jacket on, put the skis on my feet, and took hold of the rope that was attached to the boat. When the boat started to move, I began rising out of the water. But then my feet started spreading apart, and I went back down and let go of the rope. The other kids were yelling to the driver to stop, because I had fallen. The boat circled around to get me, and after I grabbed a hold of the rope, we started moving again. I heard my peers yelling, "Arta, keep your feet together! Keep your feet together! You can do it!" I fell many times before I finally mastered the fine art of water skiing. The words of encouragement from my peers gave me the courage to keep trying. They all knew how to ski, and they used their knowledge to teach me.

That's what mentoring is all about — using our knowledge to teach others. We all have valuable life experiences to share with the people around us. The mentor I had when I began my nursing career was a godsend. She was able to transfer her knowledge to me and give me a boost of confidence when I needed it. She allowed me to ask questions and she provided words of encouragement. I never doubted that she was in my cheering section.

Beulah was there when I called a doctor for the first time to get orders. I was nervous, but she practiced with me by pretending to be the physician. She stood next to me and gave me the confidence I needed to make that phone call. Beulah helped me learn to trust my instincts. I became a better nurse because of her mentoring. Whenever I teach other nurses, I think of Beulah and try to pass on her wonderful gift.

We all have something to give. We all have something to teach. We can teach someone young or old. It can be done at work, at home, through the Big Brothers/Big Sisters program, or through some other avenue. Becoming a mentor is one gift you can give that will last a lifetime.

What do you enjoy doing?
Won't you give this wonderful gift to someone?

These Are the
only feet I've got

To take no notice of a violent attack is to strengthen the heart of the enemy. Vigor is valiant, but cowardice is vile.
—Ancient Egyptian

My maternal grandparents had twelve children. One can only imagine how lively that household must have been. The following is a true story that happened when my uncle was a little boy. Uncle A.D. was going out to play. My grandmother (who we called "Madear") looked at him and said, "Your shoes are on the wrong feet." He replied, "But, these are the only feet I've got."

A funny yet provocative statement that reminds me that we need to use what we have. Sometimes it is easy to say or think that we can't do something because we are not smart enough, talented enough, rich enough, or pretty enough. Instead of thinking about what we don't have, we need to focus on what talents (feet) we do have.

A cellist who lived in Sarajevo during the war provides a good example of this. In the spring of 1992, war was raging in Sarajevo. At 4 P.M. one afternoon a bomb fell, killing twenty-two people and injuring several others. A man who once played for the Sarajevo Orchestra was broken-hearted when he saw the death and destruction from his apartment window. He wanted to do something, but what could he do? He wasn't a soldier. He wasn't a politician. He didn't have any fancy words to console the people. All he knew how to do was play the cello. How could a cellist stop a bomb? Regardless, he felt moved to action, so the next day at 4 P.M. he dressed in his work clothes — black tie and tails — took his stand, sheet music, and cello, and began to play on the corner where the bomb had fallen. He played on that corner for twenty-two days, one day for each person who was killed.

An interesting thing happened. When he played on the corner, no bombs were dropped. The pilots flying missions overhead avoided that corner when the cellist was playing. Word spread among the musicians, and they began to take turns playing music on that corner. The bombers stayed away whenever music was playing.

The cello was the only feet the musician had, and he used them to make a difference in his corner of the world.

We can choose to complain about what we don't have, or we can choose to make a difference in our corner of the world by using the talents we *do* have.

Are you willing to make use of the only feet you've got?

family

The happiest place on earth
is anywhere with my family.
—nicole banks, at age eleven

True Reflection

The happiest moments of my life have been the few which I have passed at home in the bosom of my family.
—Thomas Jefferson

One afternoon I went to the store to get milk. When I returned there was an eleven- or twelve-year-old boy playing with my children. As I walked toward the house, Nehemiah said, "Mom, I'd like you to meet my new friend. I met him yesterday and invited him to come over to meet you."

I stopped to say hello, and as I proceeded to the house, I heard my son say, "Isn't she pretty?"

His friend replied, "Yes, she is. Can I see her again?"

Nehemiah said, "Mom, can you turn around? My friend wants to see you."

I shook my head no because I was crying. I have thought many things about myself, but pretty is not one of those thoughts. My son thinks his mother is beautiful. That's how I felt about my mother. I thought she was the prettiest mother in the neighborhood. Had I really reached such high esteem with my own children?

The people who know me better than anyone else love me and think I am beautiful despite my imperfections. That day I saw my true reflection, a reflection that no mirror can ever compete with.

Don't be fooled by what the mirror shows you. Look into the eyes of those you love and those who love you, and you will see your true reflection.

Can you see yourself through the eyes of others?

who's on your team?

Though one may be overpowered, two can defend themselves. A cord of three strands is not quickly broken.
—Ecclesiastes 4:12

People seem baffled by large families. Since I have six children (including one with special needs) I am often asked how I make it through each day, I will share a true story that helps explain how we do just that.

Last year on one of our trips to Rocky Mountain National Park (we go several times a year), we were looking for a particular waterfall we had seen on a postcard. We had been at the park all day, and every waterfall we encountered, we had seen before.

Finally, we looked at the map and decided to try one more place before heading home. It turned out to be the right spot. We placed four-year-old Karmen in the stroller (because she is unable to walk) and gathered up her IV bag, diaper bag, and medications.

We discovered the trail was a little more than half a mile. I can walk one mile in about fifteen minutes, so I figured that with six kids in tow, it would take us about thirty minutes. There were people sitting at the beginning of the trailhead, and after looking at me and Karmen's loaded-down stroller, they said, "You're going up there with that?!?!"

"Yes," I replied, and they laughed and said, "Good luck!"

The kids and I looked at each other, smiled, and began pushing. We soon found out that the trail was rocky and uphill all the way. It was definitely not intended for a stroller, but we were determined to get to that waterfall. As we walked, some people observed us with pity, others gave smiles of encouragement, and some made comments such as "You're nuts!" and "You sure are one brave lady!"

We found the stroller difficult to push and stopped many times to rest. When one of us grew tired, someone else took over. At last we found a bench where we could rest. We were tired and felt like we had been climbing all day. We started asking the people coming down from the waterfall how much further we had to go. One person said, "You're almost there." Another said, "You still have a quarter of a mile left." And someone else said, "You have a mile left."

I was tired and discouraged and hungry. I wanted to turn around and go home. I gathered the kids and asked for a vote. Should we turn around and go back or should we continue to the waterfall? I was out-voted, so we headed for the waterfall. It turned out to be right around the corner, and it was beautiful. I was glad I had been out-voted!

My children and I work as a team, and in doing so we are able to accomplish things we could never accomplish alone. People may say discouraging things to us, but we keep our heads up high and re-mind each other that hard work ends in beautiful rewards.

Sometimes in this life the battles are uphill and the roads are rocky. We need to avoid people who discourage us. We need people in our lives who will encourage us and remind us that hard work will bring us a reward.

Who's on your team?

LEAVE THEM
WITH LOVING WORDS

A word aptly spoken
is like apples of gold in settings of silver.
—PROVERBS 25:11

One evening, I went to the kitchen to retrieve a map I had placed on the kitchen table earlier in the day. I was preparing to go see a patient in his home and was not familiar with the area of town where he lived. But when I went to the table, the map was nowhere in sight. I looked on the chairs and on the floor around the table, but to no avail. The longer I searched, the madder I got. I kept thinking, "I know I've told them not to move my stuff. If I find out who did it, they will be in *big* trouble." Finally I yelled for the kids to come and help me look. I told them how angry I was because I was going to be late for work and how disappointed I was that they had moved my map. They were upset when I was finished.

One of the kids said, "But Mom, we were only trying to help. We cleaned so that you wouldn't have to do it all by yourself." I felt terrible that I had been so mean, but I did not express this to my children because I was running late and needed to find the map so I could go to work.

We all searched high and low for that map and could not find it. Finally, I remembered that I had another map, and I used it to prepare for my trip.

On my way to the patient's home, I kept thinking about the encounter I had had with my children. I felt badly about getting so upset. They were only trying to fulfill a request I had made the day before. At the time I was exhausted and looked around the house at the clutter everywhere, the piled-up laundry, scattered toys, and the unmade dinner. I told my kids, "I can't do this all myself. There are seven people who made this mess, and one person can't clean it all up. I really need your help." They had all agreed to help keep the house clean.

As I drove to my appointment, I saw their sweet faces hanging low when I told them how disappointed I was in them. I was so ashamed of myself. I decided to apologize to them when I got home.

My visit with my patient took longer than I had expected, and the kids were in bed when I got home. They had gone to bed thinking that I was upset with them. I knew how horrible that must have felt. I did not sleep well that night.

The next morning, I found out that my kids hadn't slept well either. They were thinking about how they had disappointed me. I decided then that I would never go to bed angry or let my kids go to bed thinking that I was angry with them. I also decided never to leave the house if there was unresolved conflict. I kept thinking that I could have died before I made it home to say, "I'm sorry." Would I really want them to remember me as the mother who they disappointed?

Anything can happen to any of us at any time. We need to leave our loved ones with loving words.

What loving words will you leave your loved ones with each day?

one child
at a time

Call it a clan, call it a network, call it a tribe, call it a family. Whatever you call it, whoever you are, you need one.
—Jan Howard

In 1992, my adoption social worker invited me to an adoption party sponsored by The Adoption Exchange. I had just adopted my second child, an eight-month-old little boy, and was not interested in adopting again. But I wanted the children waiting for homes to know they were loved and cared about, so I decided that attending the party would be a good way to show them my support.

I took Katie (age three) and baby Kaleb, and we mingled with the kids. There was face painting, pizza, clowns twisting balloons into different shapes, games for the kids, and lots of laughter. We had a blast.

The next day I received a call from my social worker. Another social worker who had attended the party had a five- and seven-year-old sibling pair in need of a family. The children's social worker thought I would be perfect for them. Was I interested?

I agreed to speak with the social worker because I felt a connection to all the children we had met at the party. We set up an appointment for the following week to talk about the children. In the meantime, I had a lot of thinking to do. I called various social workers and asked about the effects of adopting out of birth order since these children were older than Katie. Most of the social workers told me that I could adopt any child I wanted in any order, but they asked why I wanted to adopt older children with problems associated with previous abuse. My answer was, "Why not?"

Each day I struggled to find the right answers. I found myself going back and forth. Should I adopt them or not? Did I have the skills to handle a child who might have learning disabilities? Would my extended family be able to accept a child who might never be able to attend college? Could I *really* handle four children as a single parent? The answer came to me the night before I met with the social worker.

I had tucked my two little ones into bed, read a little bit, and finally fallen asleep. At about 1 A.M., my phone rang. It was my sister. She was having boyfriend problems and needed to talk. While she was talking to me, she kept repeating, "I want to talk to Mom, but it's too early in the morning."

By then it was two in the morning, and I realized it wasn't me she wanted to talk to at all, so I finally said, "Toni, mothers are always on call. It's never too early or too late."

We hung up the phone so she could call our mother, and I went back to sleep. About two hours later, Katie's voice woke me up. She was crying, "Mommy, Mommy."

When I got to Katie's room, she said, "I just needed a hug." I obediently gave her the much-needed hug. Walking back to my room, I thought, "That's strange. She's never done that before,"

I drifted back to sleep and had a vivid dream: two children were crying, "Mommy, Mommy," and nobody came.

I immediately sat up in bed and knew that I had my answer. I was going to adopt the two children.

It didn't matter what the social worker told me at that meeting, those children belonged to me. We were a family, and we would deal with whatever "problems" they had.

Nehemiah and Nicole came home three months after that initial meeting with their social worker. Our beginning was a challenge, but my decision to adopt them is one that I have never regretted. I love them with a love that only a mother knows.

When I think about how we got together, I think of The Adoption Exchange — an organization that began with a group of social workers volunteering their lunch hour to exchange information about the children in their caseload who need a family. This group of social workers reminds me of a famous quote by Margaret Mead: "Never doubt that a small group of thoughtful committed citizens can change the world, indeed it is the only thing that ever has."

If this small group of social workers had not acted on their concern for children in the foster care system who need families, The Adoption Exchange would not exist and I would have never met Nehemiah and Nicole. The act of a few people gave my children a chance to be a part of a family. It changed their world.

The adoption of children in the foster care system does, indeed, change the world. It is the most basic way of breaking the cycle of abuse — not just for them, but for *their* children. Adoption allows foster children to learn how to love and how to be good parents. Their children are born into families with loving grandparents, aunts, uncles, and cousins, giving the new babies a chance that the children in the foster care system never had. It is remarkable. It changes lives. It changes the world!

You may be thinking, as I once did, that adopting these children is something that you do not have the skills to do, but think again. Consider this poem written by a twelve-year-old in the foster care system.

ALONE

As I sit here with my thoughts
I wonder why
I will face the world alone
Until I die.
My heart is full of sadness
Feeling sorry for myself
For I've no one to love me,
No, not even myself.
Everybody has a someone,
Everybody has a home.
Nobody knows the feeling
Of what it's like to be alone.
Life seems to work
For everyone but me.

family

> I'm loving someone,
> But that someone doesn't love me.
> I really wish I had a family,
> I really wish I had a home.
> I really wish I had a someone,
> So that I wouldn't be alone.
> —by Chris, age twelve, a foster child

You can and should do something about the children who are waiting to be adopted. You can also help families that have already adopted children from the foster care system. If you can't become an adoptive parent yourself, you can volunteer to help The Adoption Exchange find families who do want to adopt; you can offer respite (a short break from the day to day responsibility of parenting) to adoptive families; you can provide encouragement and moral support for adoptive children as they grow up and learn to be good citizens; and you can donate money to help connect children with families.

These children do not belong to the government — they belong to all of us. There is no substitute for having your own family, where you are safe from harm and where you can be loved and nurtured.

Together, we can change a life, one child at a time. And together, we can change the world.

How will you help?

For more information on The Adoption Exchange, see the appendix.

A Love Story

*There is no difficulty
that enough love will not conquer;
no disease that enough love will not heal;
no door that enough love will not open;
no gulf that enough love will not bridge;
no wall that enough love will not throw down;
no sin that enough love will not redeem.*

—Emmet Fox

In August 1997 my youngest brother, Anthony, left Denver and moved back to our hometown (Baton Rouge, Louisiana) to attend graduate school. The day he left was among the saddest my family has had to endure. He came by our house to give everyone hugs, kisses, and words of love.

After his departure I went to my room, because I was trying to keep from crying. Katie found me there, crawled into bed with me, and said, "Mommy, do you know how much Uncle Anthony loves me?"

I turned to face her and asked, "How much does Uncle Anthony love you?"

"This much," she said and pressed her thumb and index finger as close together as she could get them. Then she added, "This is how close we are. Nothing can ever come between us!" I smiled, because it brought me back to a time long ago.

I remembered the day my mother told us she was going to have a baby. I was eight-years-old, my sister was seven, and my brother was almost six. We were so excited! My mother was in shock; all of her kids were finally in school — how did this happen?!?!? (Well, we all know how it happened. I think the real question may have been: Why?)

The shock soon wore off, and as her belly grew so did our anticipation. My sister and I prayed for a boy so that our brother could have someone close to him, like she and I had each other. Each day when my mother came home from work, my sister would massage her swollen feet. Even though my mother never asked her to do this, she wanted to as an expression of love for our mother and the baby.

On August 31, 1973, the Greatest Surprise ever was born, and my parents named him Anthony. My siblings and I felt like he was our baby, but I especially felt like he was mine. I felt like I was sharing mothering.

One night when I heard him crying, I got up, fed him, and then held him and walked around and around our coffee table until he fell asleep. This became our ritual until he finally started to sleep through the night at four-months-old. It was my way of expressing my love for my mother and baby brother. That first time though, my mom got up the next morning and told my dad the baby had slept all night. My dad replied that she was the only baby who had slept all night!

My siblings and I taught him everything we knew and loved him unconditionally, so when I graduated from high school and left home to attend college, I was very worried about my baby brother. We shared a strong and unique bond. Who was going to take my place and provide this for him? I wrote him often and missed him dearly.

Because I missed him so much, I asked my mother if he could spend his spring break with me at my college. She assented, and my brother spent an entire week with me on campus and went to classes and chapel with me every day.

We had a blast. My friends fell in love with him. When the week ended, it was sad for both of us. On the morning that he was to leave, we walked on campus hand in hand. Neither of us said a word. What do you say when you feel like your heart is being ripped out?

We came to a swing on campus and sat down. I looked at Anthony and said, "Anthony, do you know how much I love you?"

"How much do you love me?" he asked.

"This much," I said and pressed my thumb and forefinger as close together as I could get them. "This is how close we are. Nothing can ever come between us. It does not matter where you are or where I am, I always will love you. A zillion miles is nothing compared to the love we share." With those words both of us felt better, and there was no need for tears.

I had never spoken those words since, and my brother and I had not mentioned our conversation again. So when Katie said the words I had spoken thirteen years earlier, I couldn't believe my brother had remembered, and I felt no need for tears. The words of love that had comforted an eleven year old boy now brought comfort to my children and me. At that moment I understood 1 Corinthians 13:13 "And now these three remain: faith, hope, and love. But the greatest of these is love."

In the end, nothing else will matter. It will not matter how much money you made, what kind of clothes you wore, the type of house you lived in, how far up the corporate ladder you climbed, or how pretty you were. The only thing that will matter is love — who you loved and who loved you. Doesn't that make life a whole lot simpler? Love is a four-letter word full of power.

Take a moment today to do something that *really* matters: hug your child, call someone you should have called yesterday, listen to your spouse, have dinner together, fix the kids breakfast in bed, smile, kiss, hold hands, and say, "I love you." When the day is done, you'll be glad you did those things. When the end has come, as it does for each of us, love is the thing we will remember most.

How will you express your love today?

the gift of time

It will be gone before you know it.
The fingerprints on the wall appear higher and higher.
Then suddenly they disappear.
—Dorothy Evslin

When I was sixteen, I babysat for the ladies' Bible class that my mom co-led. One day while I was babysitting, my dad called. One of his co-workers had concert tickets, and he needed to know if our busy teenage schedules could accommodate the activity.

When I got off the phone, one of the girls I was babysitting said, "Tay-tay, who was that?"

"That was my dad. He wanted to know if my siblings and I wanted to go to a concert with him."

The three-year-old girl became quiet and her face looked sad. I picked her up, placed her on my knee, and said, "What's wrong?" When she did not answer, I said, "Please tell me what's wrong; I can't help you if I don't know."

She replied, "If I tell you what's wrong, you have to promise not to tell." I promised.

" I wish my dad would play with me," she said, burying her head in my shoulder to cry. I told her how much her daddy loved her. She said, "I know he loves me. I just want to play with him."

I kept her secret for many years. Now that she is older, I feel compelled to share this story, because as parents we need to be reminded of what is really important.

Our children want *us* more than they want new toys, fancy clothes, or dancing lessons. When we choose to give our children things rather than time, we cheat them as well as ourselves.

My greatest childhood memories are those of spending time with my parents. My mother taught me how to play jacks, pump a swing, and jump rope. My dad taught me karate, the difference between left and right, and my multiplication tables. I remember dancing with my parents before they went to a ball. Whenever I think of those times, I smile. I dance with my children often.

The greatest gift we can give our children is our time. They need that gift, and we also will reap great rewards by giving it to them. Let's not only tell our children that we love them, let's show them that we love them by giving them our time.

What would you like to do with your child today?

dreams & courage

---

*After seeing a piano in our living room,
a guest asked my son if he knew how to play.
He replied, "I don't know.
I've never tried."*

—Nehemiah Banks, at age nine

follow your Heart

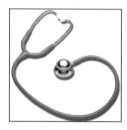

If a man does not keep pace with his companions, perhaps it is because he hears a different drummer. Let him step to the music which he hears, however measured or far away.

—Henry David Thoreau

At the ripe old age of seventeen, I decided I was tired of people telling me what to do. I graduated a semester early from high school and began my college career at Louisiana State University. Even though the university was in my hometown of Baton Rouge, I decided to live in the dorms.

That first semester on campus was quite an adjustment. I had never seen anyone drunk before arriving on campus, but I saw someone drunk every night after I moved in. I grew up in a family that valued education so I didn't understand people flunking out of school and losing scholarships for the sake of partying. It did not make sense to me. The number of girls who used abortion as birth control was also a shock to me. But the biggest shock, by far, was watching girls who thought they were still virgins find out that they were not because they had a positive pregnancy test. While trying to fit in, they used drugs and alcohol and were abused while they were impaired.

I wanted to fit in too, but the price was higher than I was willing to pay.

I called my mother, in tears, at 3 A.M. one morning and asked her why she hadn't told me about the *real* world. I felt like a foreigner who had not learned the customs and language of the country.

There was one place where I still fit in: my home congregation. I continued to be active there, and I also continued to visit a woman from my church who had been diagnosed with cancer. Each week I went home and borrowed the family car to go visit her. As she became sicker, visiting her became more difficult. Eventually I stopped going.

One day, she sent a messenger to my dorm room with a message for me. The message was this: "Arta, I know you're afraid, and it's okay." A woman in pain from her cancer and struggling to live was worried about me. I knew I needed to go see her.

The next day, I again borrowed the family car and went to see her. When I walked into her house, I asked how she was doing, but she didn't want to talk about herself. She wanted to talk about me. Sensing that this was important to her, I told her about college life. She listened with much interest. I also told her about my struggle with my family over my choice of careers. Everyone expected me to go to medical school, but I had decided to become a nurse, because the flexibility of nursing would make it possible for me to realize my dream of adopting children as a single mom.

After I had finished talking, she cradled my face in her hands and said, "Arta, we all know how smart you are. If you want to go to medical school, you can do that. You may even find a cure for cancer. In your heart you know what is right to do. Follow your heart."

Those words, "In your heart you know what is right," gave me the courage to do what I needed. In the dorms, I was able to embrace the people around me without betraying my conscience. I didn't need to abuse my body with drugs or alcohol to fit in. I became the "ear" that many girls needed to help them face the consequences of their actions. I was also able to face my family and friends with my decision to become a nurse. It is a decision I have never regretted.

Many of you may have people in your life who disagree with your dreams and goals. Listen to my friend's advice. In your heart you know what is right to do. Follow your heart.

What is your heart telling you?

keep your dreams in view

You must have long range goals to keep you from being frustrated by short range failure.

—charles c. noble

As a child, my grandmother's rocking chair was the center of my life. Her children, grandchildren, and great-grandchildren sat at her feet as she shared her wisdom and humor with us. We listened to her hum spirituals, trying to wait patiently as she peeled apples for us to eat, and we shared our dreams with her. She always had the magic words that made us feel like we could conquer the world. The time spent at the foot of her rocking chair was special to her family. This story is just one example why.

I was eight years old when I decided that I wanted to adopt. Every decision I made after that was based on making that dream a reality. I was a good student with an interest in medicine, but chose nursing over becoming a physician because I believed the flexibility of nursing would be more compatible with my dream of adopting children. When I graduated from college, I moved to Oklahoma. I was on the phone getting an application to adopt before I had unloaded the U-haul!

On my first trip home from Oklahoma, I began telling people about my plans to adopt. I think people thought I was asking for their permission because I received a number of lectures. I was frustrated by this unsolicited advice, but I did not let it discourage me. When I told my grandmother that I was going to adopt a little girl, she looked at me and said, "Arta, you are going to be a good mother, but if you want to wear expensive clothes, you need to do that before the children come."

I replied, "I have worn expensive clothes and I was not impressed."

She just smiled and said, "If you want to buy expensive jewelry, you need to do it before you adopt."

I answered, "I have owned expensive jewelry, and I lost it."

Then she said, "If you want to travel to Europe, you need to do it before you become a mother."

I told her, "If I traveled anywhere, it would not be Europe. I would go to Central and South America. When I go, I want to go with kids in tow. I want them to fall in love with the culture."

"Madear," I added, "I am worried about spoiling my children. I do not want children that no one can stand to be around."

She said, "The only way not to spoil a child is to not love the child, but you must teach your children that not everything belongs to them. When you have children, do not put your nice things away. Teach your children that there are things they are not to touch. If you teach them that in your own home, they will not touch things when they go to other people's houses, and they will always be welcomed back."

She paused for a moment and waited for me to process all the information she had given me. Then she said, "It does not matter if your children come to you by adoption or if you give birth to them, the love you have for them is the same. I know. I've done both. Arta, you will be a good mother."

Her words fed my soul. She supported me when most people thought I was crazy. I think she understood my need to do what I was called to do, because she had once had a calling and a dream too.

When my grandparents got married, on December 17, 1936, they naturally began making plans for their life together. One of their dreams was for all of their children to go to college. Because of their Native-American and African-American heritage, their dream was viewed as an impossible one (especially in the South). Nevertheless, everything they did focused on making this dream a reality.

One day I asked my grandmother how she came to dream such a dream for her family. She said, "The university was right across the street. I could see it from my house." The university was right across the street — the dream was always in view.

My grandparents had twelve children, and yes, they all went to college. Among them there are engineers, a doctor, a law student, entrepreneurs, educators, certified public accountants, an Air Force Senior Master Sergeant, and corporate supervisors. The effects of my grandparents' dream have been felt in the generations that followed. I always thought your education was not complete until you graduated from college. I never considered other options, as some do, because I didn't realize that there were other options available. My cousins had the same point of view on this matter that I had.

An impossible dream was made possible by keeping it in view.

What are you dreaming about? Are people laughing at your dreams? Are you feeling unsure of your ability to make your dreams a reality? Well, heed my grandmother's words: "If you can think it, you can do it!"

Always keep your dreams before you, and you will succeed. Believe in your dreams and they will become a reality.

What is your dream?

Lessons I Learned while sitting at My Grandmother's feet

You can't get your blessings with your hands closed.
You have to give in order to receive.
—Clara Byrd Square

The following are life lessons I have learned. These are written in loving memory of Clara Byrd Square, affectionately known as "Madear", February 28, 1917– April 6, 1999

1. Children always come first, so if you want to wear expensive clothes, buy expensive jewelry, or travel to Europe, do it before the children come.

2. Always be thankful.

3. When times are tough, laughter is good medicine.

4. If someone is suffering from the consequences of their actions or choices, don't rub it in. (They already know their mistake.) Offer comfort, love, and support instead.

5. If you disagree with a choice a friend or a family member has made, speak your piece and then shut up and stand by them anyway. Their decision may be based on information you are not privy to.

6. You don't need to prove your worthiness to anyone, because when you were born, you were born *somebody*.

7. Children belong to all of us. Protect them.

8. If people mistreat you, it doesn't mean they don't love you. It may be the only way they know how to love.

9. The greatest pain in life is when a mother loses her child. Life goes on, but the pain remains.

10. Always keep your dreams before you and you will succeed.

11. If you can think it, you can do it!

12. Education is important because it gives you a brighter future.

13. Be thankful for the good times, but be prepared for whatever may come along by keeping money in the bank and food in your freezer.

14. When you go on a job interview, wear your black suit or your navy blue suit.

15. When you go to work, keep your personal business to yourself and look forward to two days: payday and day off.

16. Children are *supposed* to ask questions.

17. The pain of name-calling stays with people forever, so don't do it.

18. Families should stick together. When you have a disagreement, the *only* choice you have is to work it out.

19. You can't get your blessings with your hands closed. You have

to give in order to receive.

20. The letter "f" is a crooked letter and you can't make it straight. You can't "if" your way through life.

21. The only way to not spoil a child is to not love the child.

22. When someone dies, they are making room for new family members.

What values or lessons would you like to leave with the next generation?

facing fear

Most of our obstacles would melt away if, instead of cowering before them, we should make up our minds to walk boldly through them.

—orison swett marden

My siblings and I were lucky enough to grow up in the same city as both sets of our grandparents, and we enjoyed spending time with them. Our maternal grandparents had land as far as our little eyes could see, a playhouse our grandfather built for us, a fenced-in yard, and plenty of room for imagination. We only had two rules while we were there: do not chase the chickens, and do not play with the outside water faucet.

One Saturday morning, my cousin, siblings, and I were playing at my grandparent's house and were in a mischievous mood. We knew that if we chased the chickens, we would get caught because of all the noise they make. So we decided to play in the water. Just as we turned on the faucet, my grandfather came out. At six-feet, four-inches tall, he could intimidate anyone — but especially five- to seven-year-olds! We were scared because we had disobeyed, and we all started running as fast as our legs would carry us. Our cousin lived next door, and that's where we headed. As we were going through the gate, between the houses, my uncle passed by. Since he's also over six-feet tall, most of us were able to run through his legs or around him, but he caught my brother.

The rest of us got to my cousin's house and hid under his bed. We were so scared. We knew we had done something wrong and deserved to be punished. We were also worried about my brother. What would they do to him? Was he all right?

We spent all day under that bed. We finally came out because we were starving. Hunger made us brave. When we went back to my grandparents' house, my brother was smiling and having a good time. My uncle had carried him on his shoulders all day long, and he had been treated like a king. We had spent the day in misery because of fear. My brother had faced it (voluntarily or not!) and been rewarded.

Many of us stay in bad relationships, jobs we hate, or situations that are uncomfortable or unhealthy because of fear. We're afraid of the unknown, but we must remember that things cannot get better unless we are willing to face the fear. Eleanor Roosevelt is known for the following quote: "You gain strength, courage, and confidence by every experience in which you stop to look fear in the face…we must do that which we think we cannot."

Isn't it time for you to stop letting fear control you? You may be surprised to find good things waiting for you. Who knows? It may be your turn to be treated like royalty.

Do you have any fears you need to face?

watermelon rind

All the ingredients that you need to succeed in this world are within reach.

When I was a child, summertime and watermelon went hand in hand. My mother would cut the watermelon and send us to the backyard to eat it. I remember being worried about swallowing a seed, because I thought a watermelon would grow in my belly! I had heard that from another child. It is amazing how impressionable I was.

It was silly to believe what I had heard about a watermelon growing in my belly, but I did learn an important and not-so-silly lesson from a watermelon. It happened on a summer afternoon when I was nine years old.

My dad had the day off from work, so he was caring for my siblings and me. He cut watermelon for us, and, instead of sending us outside like my mother usually did, he had us sit at the kitchen table.

As we ate the watermelon, he cooked dinner. When we got up to throw our watermelon rinds away, my dad told us how they made dessert out of watermelon rind when he was a kid. We gave him that "yeah, right" look! We thought he was just telling us another story — like the ones about walking barefoot to school in the snow.

My dad knew we didn't believe him, so he decided to show us he was telling the truth. He took our watermelon rind and began cutting it into small pieces. He placed the rind into a big pot of water, added several spices, and placed a lid on the pot. It took a few hours for the watermelon rind to cook. Periodically my dad checked on the rind to see if it was soft enough to eat, and he added more spices.

When the watermelon rind dessert was done, my dad called us in to taste it. It was the best dessert we had ever had! We couldn't believe he had made dessert out of something we were planning to throw away.

Many people are told they are not good enough, smart enough, rich enough, or pretty enough. Eventually they begin to believe the words they hear. But when you hear such things, think about the watermelon rind. To us, it was garbage; but to my father, it was dessert.

You are not garbage. Do not allow others to make you think you are. Think of my father and remember that all the ingredients you need to succeed in this world are within reach.

What negative words have you been believing?

got a map?

If you don't know where you're going
any road will take you there.

One December, when Karmen was three or four years old, our family was in Baton Rouge, Louisiana, visiting relatives. The night before we were to return to Colorado, Karmen became ill. She had a temperature of a 102°, and I was up most of the night with her. About an hour before we planned to leave she fell asleep, and I followed suit. When I woke up, my brother Artie was standing over me because he wanted to know if I needed help driving home. I explained that Karmen was sick, and that I was tired, but I wanted to get her to Colorado so she could see her own doctors. He offered to drive us back to Colorado — a twenty-four-hour road trip!

We packed the car and the children and were on our way. As the children talked and slept, Artie drove, and I held Karmen's hand while she cried. I gave her Tylenol® and ibuprofen to no avail. We were about fourteen hours into the trip when I noticed drainage coming from Karmen's ear. I felt relieved to know that she had an ear infection — something normal — and not an infection related to her HIV - status.

Karmen soon fell asleep for the first time in more than fourteen hours. My brother did not know the directions, but I knew that we would be on this particular interstate highway for a few more hours. I decided to nap while he drove and Karmen slept.

About five hours later, I woke up and didn't recognize where we were. Thinking that I was just blurry-eyed from sleeping, I rubbed my eyes. It did not help. I looked at my brother and asked, "Where are we?"

We were in a town that I had never heard of — two hours out of our way. I had been sleeping when it was time to change interstate highways. Since this was his first trip from Baton Rouge to Denver, he did not know where to turn. There was no map in the car, because I had made this trip so many times that I knew it by heart.

Artie felt terrible. He had volunteered to help me drive home so we could get Karmen to the doctor faster, and he had gotten us lost instead. I knew it was an honest mistake and that I was responsible, too. We stopped at the nearest gas station and bought a map. After studying the map, we discovered that turning around was not the fastest way to get home. We needed to take a highway that would eventually connect us to the correct interstate, I-70.

I took over the task of driving while Artie slept. Since we were driving on a state highway instead of an interstate, we had to go fifty-five miles per hour, rather than the sixty-five to seventy-five miles per hour we were accustomed to — and we had to slow down when we got to small towns or found ourselves behind a tractor!

Eventually, we found our way back to I-70 and made it to Denver. Our course was not the one we had planned, but, because we knew where we wanted to go, we were able to get there. We recognized that although we were lost, we could change our direction to reach our final destination.

This is true in life, as well. For us to reach our destination in life, we need to know exactly where we want to go. We need to have a goal. Once we've decided on a goal, we can figure out how to get there — that's the map. My brother Anthony credits one of his graduate school professors with this bit of wisdom, "If you don't know where you're going, any road will take you there."

Have you ever looked around and found yourself saying, "Where am I? Dear God, how did I get in this mess?" Those questions are good ones. It means you recognize you are off course. Once you make that determination, you can change your map to get yourself back on course. It may take a little more time, but eventually you will reach your goal.

Do you know where you are headed?

Dreaming Dreams

If there were dreams to sell, what would you buy?
—Thomas L. Beddoses

If your life was to flash before you right now, what would you like to see? What kinds of things would you like to do or learn? Try to list a hundred things and be sure to list them without judging whether they are possible. It may take you several weeks to complete this, but if you take the time to do it, you will find several new things to look forward to!

In your journal or a notebook, list one hundred things you desire to do.

inside-out day

*There are many paths to the top of the mountain,
but the view is always the same.*

—chinese proverb

My first child, Kathryn Da'Lynn, was named after two wonderful women who have taught me a great deal about being a good mother. This story is about one of those lessons.

When my daughter Katie was two-and-one-half years old, we went to Virginia to visit Kathy, my pen pal since I was fifteen, and her family. One evening after dinner, we decided to go out for dessert. We had been playing hard all day, so everyone decided to change clothes before we left. Katie and I were among the first people ready. When we went into the den, Becka (Kathy's two-year-old) had on her shirt inside out and backwards (the tag was visible under her chin), her pants on backwards, and her brother's boots, which were three or four sizes too big and on the wrong feet! I thought she looked cute, but since we were going out in public I decided to tell her mother so she could correct the situation.

I found Kathy and told her, "You need to check on Becka." Kathy looked at me with a "what could be wrong with Becka that you couldn't handle?" look.

I explained that Becka's clothes were inside out and that her shoes were on the wrong feet. Kathy looked at me gently and with a kind and patient voice she said, "The world will tell my child that her shoes are on the wrong feet and that her clothes don't match. When she comes home, she needs to find love and acceptance. I won't tell my child that her clothes are on wrong, but you can!"

I went into the den and put Becka and Katie on my lap and read them a story until everyone else was ready to go. I had no desire to be the big, bad world!

Before we went for dessert, we stopped by the hospital because George (Kathy's husband) was concerned about a patient he had admitted that day. When George, Kathy, their three children, Katie and I went into the patient's room, I could see why George was concerned. His patient was an elderly woman, and she was so scared that the bed actually looked like it was swallowing her. When her doctor walked in with his family and friends, her face lit up. If she noticed Becka's attire, she did not mention it. We talked to her and the children lavished her with hugs. I think she was having an inside-out, wrong-feet kind of day, too. But in us, she found the love and acceptance that she needed to fill that bed up. Before we left, Becka gave her a kiss on the cheek and the smile on her face was bright enough to light the entire hospital!

We all have inside-out, wrong-feet kind of days, and when that happens we need love and acceptance to get through them.

That experience with Becka helped me remember an experience I had in the first grade. My uncle taught me how to write in cursive, and I practiced all weekend so that I could show my teacher on Monday. When I got to school, I did my schoolwork perfectly, and at the top of my page I proudly wrote my name in cursive.

When I got my paper back from my teacher, instead of the smiley face I was expecting, there was a sad face above my name. A note told me that first-graders did not write in cursive, and that from now on I had to print. I gave this teacher my very best and she rejected it.

I felt very sad that day. I left class and went into the bathroom and ripped that paper up and threw it in the trashcan. I did not tell my parents what had happened, because I knew that my father would be angry with my teacher, and seeing him angry was scary. In my room I practiced writing my name in cursive. When I was happy with the results, I brought my paper to my mother. She said, "This is the most beautiful handwriting I have ever seen."

When she said that, it did not matter what my teacher had said, because I had found the love and acceptance that I needed. All I wanted was for someone to be proud of me for learning to write my name in cursive. Because my mother gave that gift to me, I was able to forgive my teacher.

On Tuesday, I went to school with a smile on my face, and I still liked my teacher and thought that school was fun.

We all have the power to turn someone's inside-out, upside-down, wrong-feet kind of day into something beautiful by offering kindness, gentleness, love, and acceptance. We even have the power to alter our own inside-out, upside-down, wrong-feet kind of days by accepting those days and loving ourselves through them.

My wish for you is that such days are few and far between. But when they do come, I pray that you will find the love and acceptance you need to help you get through them.

How can you help others through their inside-out, wrong-feet kind of days?

afterwords

Afterword

When I was a little girl, we were often invited to spend time in other people's homes. Before we would exit the car, my mother always said, "Leave it better than you found it."

By reading this book, you have invited me into your home. My sincere wish is that this book has left you better than it found you.

If you wish to contact me:
Arta Banks c/o Lovegifts Publishing
P.O. Box 201388
Denver, CO 80220
lovegiftspub@aol.com
www.lovegiftspublishing.com

acknowledgments

This book would not have been possible without the love, friendship, financial support, and words of encouragement of many people.

Thanks to all the people who showed their support and faith in this project and in me by purchasing a book before publication or by making a donation.

Thank you, Mom, for spelling my words for me before I could spell them myself.

Thank you, Dad, for telling me that I am a Banks and that a Banks can do anything.

Kathy Tran, thanks for being my pen pal and friend for the last twenty years. You taught me that words can sing, dance, laugh, and cry.

Ackowledgments

Thanks to my children for their enthusiasm when I announced my plans to write a book. You are wonderful cheerleaders and your love makes me believe the impossible is possible.

Catherine O'Neill Thorn, thank you for editing this book. You are worth your weight in gold.

Thank you, Doug and Linda Yohn, for believing in this project and in me. You helped me believe it was possible. Linda, thanks for taking this journey with me.

Dr. Jandel T. Allen-Davis, thank you for planting the idea of a book in my head!

Katy Tartakoff and The Children's Legacy, thank you for allowing me to use the beautiful photographs in this book. Thanks also for the love and support you have provided to my family over the years.

Candy White, thanks for your enthusiasm and words of encouragement.

Elizabeth Able, thank you for being there when I needed a friend. You are a gift from God. Thanks also for your wonderful feedback on this book. Your ideas helped make this book what it is today.

Jeanie March, thank you for making Karmen's wedding dress without needing to understand why. You are a great friend.

Karen Lackie, thank you for the wonderful "lovegifts" you sent throughout my teen years. I am fortunate to have you in my life.

For the past three years, I have had the privilege of sending "lovegift" letters to the special people in my life. Because of the love and words of encouragement that I received from people on my lovegifts mailing list, this book exists. A special thanks to all of you on that list. I love you all.

I was unable to find Chris, the writer of the poem "Alone," but I want to thank him for writing such a beautiful poem. It helps the world understand what it feels like to be a waiting child.

Appendix

Organizations and Information Sources

The Adoption Exchange
14232 E. Evans Ave., Aurora, CO 80014
Voice: 303-755-4756
Toll Free: 1-800-451-5246
kids@adoptex.org
www.adoptex.org

The Adoption Exchange is not an adoption placement agency. It provides the connection between families who adopt and children who wait. They provide education and information on the adoption process, host adoption parties so that waiting children and prospective parents can meet, provide picture books of waiting children, have a list of waiting children on their web site, and have a Wednesday's child program which features waiting children on the news. The Adoption Exchange has various volunteer opportunities available.

Angel's Unaware and Camp Ray-Ray
6370 Union Street
Arvada, CO 80004
Voice: 303-420-6370
Fax: 303-456-4040
angelsunaware@att.net
www.angelsunaware.net

Camp Ray-Ray is held once a year and is sponsored by Angel's Unaware, a nonprofit organization that provides support groups for children and families affected or infected by HIV/AIDS. Support group meetings are held once a month. All services are provided to families free of charge. If you are a family in need of support or wish to make a donation please send inquiries to the address above.

The Children's Legacy
P.O. Box 300305
Denver, CO 80203
Voice: 303-830-7595
Fax: 303-860-9648
tclphoto@aol.com
www.childrenslegacy.com

The Children's Legacy (TCL) provides opportunities for families faced with life-threatening illnesses to tell their stories and celebrate their lives through photography, art, and writing. All services are provided to families free of charge. The nonprofit organization also provides education to the community through photo exhibits. If you are interested in TCL's services, wish to make a donation, or want to sponsor an exhibit in your community, please contact Katy Tartakoff or Rebecca Sophia Lee at the address or phone number listed.

The National Adoption Center

1500 Walnut St., Suite 701

Philadelphia, PA 19102

Voice: 215-735-9988

Toll Free: 1 800 To Adopt

nac@adopt.org

www.adoptnet.org

www.adopt.org

The National Adoption Center is not an adoption agency. They provide general information on the adoption process. Their website features pictures of waiting children as well as adoption resources.

ordering information

Easily order additional copies of this quality hardcover giftbook.

Please complete the form below and calculate your total.

If paying by credit cards, you may order by:

PHONE   303-537-7338

FAX   303-537-7339

EMAIL   lovegiftspub@aol.com

WEBSITE   www.lovegiftspublishing.com

If paying by check, money order, or credit card,

send check or money order payable to: *Lovegifts Publishing*

P.O. Box 201388   Denver, CO 80220

NAME

SHIP–TO ADDRESS

SHIP–TO CITY / STATE / ZIP

PHONE	EMAIL

ITEM	QUANTITY	UNIT COST	TOTAL
Wrong Feet First		$14.95	
SHIPPING & HANDLING (S&H)	1ST BOOK	$3.50	
REDUCED S&H FOR ADDITIONAL		$1.00	
COLORADO RESIDENTS TAX	(7.55%)		
		TOTAL	

CREDIT CARD (CHECK ONE)   ☐ **VISA**   ☐ **MasterCard**   ☐ **AMERICAN EXPRESS Card**   ☐ **DISCOVER**

CARD NUMBER	EXP DATE

SIGNATURE

Shipping & Handling $3.50 for first book / $1.00 for each additional.

FREE SHIPPING & HANDLING on orders of 3 books or more!

Sales tax for Colorado residents is 7.55% and is applied to S&H

(tax for first book is $1.39 / $1.20 for each additional book.)

MONEY BACK GUARANTEE

If you are not completely satisfied when you receive your book,

I will refund your money minus shipping and handling.

•Discounts offered on quantity orders•

Lovegifts